GLAD TO BE
Grey

GLAD TO BE GREY

Copyright © Clive Whichelow, 2013

Illustrations by Ian Baker

All rights reserved.

Summersdale Publishers Ltd
46 West Street
Chichester
West Sussex
PO19 1RP
UK

www.summersdale.com

Printed and bound in the Czech Republic

ISBN: 978-1-84953-453-6

Substantial discounts on bulk quantities of Summersdale books are available to corporations, professional associations and other organisations. For details contact Nicky Douglas by telephone: +44 (0) 1243 756902, fax: +44 (0) 1243 786300 or email: nicky@summersdale.com.

GLAD TO BE
Grey

CLIVE WHICHELOW

summersdale

Introduction

When you get to a certain age you may begin to wonder what you've got to look forward to. Well, the answer is – plenty!

No more trying to keep up with clothing fads. As Confucius might have said, 'If you're never in fashion, you'll never go out of fashion!'

You're beyond caring what's in the charts – unless of course it's the charts at the end of your hospital bed. And age brings with it a certain sort of innocence. Own up, did you buy *Fifty Shades of Grey* thinking it was a hairpiece catalogue?

And why do you need to know anything about technology? You probably thought the 'i' in 'iPad' stood for 'incontinence'. If the last tweet you had was from your pet budgie then this is the book for you.

So, chins up! Put away that hair dye, get that twinkle back behind your varifocals and enjoy yourself. In short, be glad to be grey! You know it makes sense.

Why Fashion Doesn't Matter Anymore

In the evenings, youngsters have to decide whether to wear jeans, skirts, trousers, leggings, jeggings, meggings… And you? You just have to decide which jim-jams to put on

The only tattoo you're ever likely to
pay for is the Edinburgh Tattoo

You thought Gok Wan was a big
frying-pan thing for cooking noodles

Why TV Is Better When You're Older

You've now seen so much TV you can enjoy endless games of 'Oh, what was he/she in back in the 1960s/70s/80s?'

It's a little-known secret that all the best programmes are on during the day when everyone else is at work

You can happily watch TV for hours without remembering you've seen most of the programmes before

The Advantages Of Not Having To Use A Computer

The last time you were deluged
with spam was at school dinners

Being 'defriended' on Facebook
holds no horrors for you – in fact
it could well make your day

The Advantages Of Not Depending On A Mobile Phone

Your idea of recharging your batteries is with a stiff gin and tonic

You don't have to 'remember to switch off' every time you go to see a film or to the library

You can still remember how to spell words such as 'great' properly

You don't have to constantly check your phone for messages – if someone wants you the phone will ring!

Why You Prefer Books To E-Readers

You can chuck your Dan Brown at your other half, without causing £100 worth of damage

Books don't run out of batteries

How else can you impress
your friends if your shelves
of highbrow literature aren't
gracing the living room?

Hair Decisions You No Longer Have To Make (Women)

Whether to grow it long again –
you'll only look like a bag-lady

Whether to have a crop – you'll be
mistaken for your other half

Hair Decisions You No Longer Have To Make (Men)

Midlife crisis ponytail? Come on, even Francis Rossi from Status Quo doesn't have one any more!

To gel or not to gel? Perhaps superglue might be best

The chances of teasing and gelling your three remaining hairs into a Mohican are, frankly, non-existent

Why You'll Never Be Arrested

You're too unfit to be considered
capable of breaking and entering

You're too poor to be suspected
as an embezzler

These days it's more likely that it's
the bank who's robbing you!

The only money you've laundered is
when you left a ten-pound note in
your trousers before washing them

Why A Bad
Memory Is Good

If you fail to remember enough
passwords, you'll never have
to do anything on a computer
ever again – yippee!

Eventually, all those people you owe
money will tire of asking for it back

It saves a small fortune on Christmas cards

Eventually your spouse will give up asking
you to pick things up from the supermarket

The Advantages Of Not Understanding Teenage Slang

You can ignore grandchildren's hints for expensive presents because they have deemed them 'sick', indicating to you that they don't want them

You will be blissfully unaware when
a 'hoodie' is being rude to you

You greet any encouragement to 'LOL' as
an excuse to loll in your favourite armchair

Things Older People Know That Youngsters Don't

Tattoos will go out of fashion, and getting rid of them is an expensive way of not looking ridiculous

After a certain point, you can't actually get any drunker

The speed limit is not intended to be the *minimum* your car should go

How Things Have Changed!

Then		Now
Boring Sunday afternoons		Peaceful Sunday afternoons
Pubs full of old people		Pubs full of friends
Annoying little ankle-biters		Lovely grandchildren
Reactionary old gits		People talking sense for a change

Why Your Social Life Is Better

It's so much cheaper to
have friends round for
drinks rather than paying
extortionate nightclub prices

You can be nicely tucked up in bed by eleven instead of just beginning your night out

MUSIC
CHATTER
LAUGHS
CHEERS

The Upside Of Not Being Slim

You couldn't wear the more extreme fashions, even if you wanted to

You can enjoy guilt-free cakes and biscuits whenever you damn well fancy

None of your friends will hate you

You don't need to check waist
sizes – just buy 'expandable'

Why It's Gr8 Not To Text

When your fingers are like
a pack of pork chipolatas,
those tiddly buttons are just
too tricky to type with

It takes so long thinking of
ways to abbreviate words that
you might as well phone

If you don't send texts, you
won't receive any. Hooray!

How You Can Still Surprise People

An 18-year-old dying their hair magenta will go unnoticed, but at your age it's a revolutionary act!

Wear a short skirt – especially effective if you're a man

Why Tweeting's For The Birds

You don't need to tell everyone
what you had for breakfast
– they can just look at the
stains on your cardie

If you want to listen to daft, pointless
comments from people you don't know
you can just sit on a bus for five minutes

If you really want to follow
Stephen Fry he's on the box
almost continuously, anyway

Why You're Less Likely To Be A Victim Of Crime

You are unlikely to be carting around £1,000 of electronic gadgetry like a teenager

Your ancient CD player and
'tiny' 22-inch TV will not be
considered black-market gold

Cyber hacking? You're not even aware
that you have a cyber to be hacked

Stalkers? Dream on!

Things You're (Thankfully) Now Too Old For

Caring what other people think – it's like being a teenager again!

Bothering to keep your weight
down – chocs away? No way!

Caring about the latest bands
(including gastric ones)

Why Your Pop Music Was Better

People didn't have daft names – well, apart from Dave Dee, Dozy, Beaky, Mick & Tich, Napoleon XIV, Tiny Tim…

You could see bands at the local palais for
two bob instead of £100 at the O2 Arena

Or, even better, free concerts
(like, groovy, man)

All your favourite bands and singers
are still going! Will Justin Bieber still be
selling out stadiums in 50 years' time?

Things You Can Now Finally Admit To

Like Bill Clinton, you never inhaled
– even when smoking cigarettes

You thought Mary Whitehouse
was quite often right

You always hated the taste
of tequila slammers

Why Holidays Are Better When You're Older

You can get up at breakfast time instead of going to bed at breakfast time

You don't have to do dangerous
water sports to impress members
of the opposite sex

You don't have to lose weight
before going on holiday

The Upside Of Dodgy Eyesight

Even your own reflection in the mirror is less wrinkled than you deserve

It's a good excuse for not doing the
housework quite as thoroughly as before

You can justify ignoring people
you don't want to talk to

Now your other half is no longer
the fresh-faced, sylph-like figure
of yore you hardly notice

The Upside Of Dodgy Hearing

The pub bore will give you up as a lost cause

You don't have to listen to your other half snoring

Someone else always has to answer the doorbell and phone

Why It's Actually Quite Good To Be Unfit

No one says to you, 'Are you feeling strong?' when there's something heavy to be lifted

You'll save a small fortune
on gym membership

The energy you save by doing nothing
will add another five years to your life

Things That Just Don't Happen When You're Young

People offering to carry
your shopping for you

Being treated as an equal by
doctors/policemen/traffic cops

People being nice to you so they'll
get included in your will

Why Your Love Life Is Better These Days

At last you're comfortable in your own skin – even if it is a bit looser

The only problems you have with dates is getting them out of the box at Christmas

You love your other half more
than ever – mainly because they're
starting to look like you

Viagra!

Why You're Financially Better Off Now

After all those years of bailing out your kids, you can now get loans from them

At a certain age, half the stuff you need is discounted, the other half is free!

Things You Can Do That Youngsters Can't

Get a huge amount of pleasure
out of merely sitting down

With Age Comes Wisdom, Such As...

If at first you don't succeed it's hardly
worth wasting your time again

Do unto others before they do it unto you

A friend in need is a friend in debt

Never take advice from anyone
who offers advice

Things You Can Now Say

Now listen here young man/young lady…

Of course, it was all different in my day…

Grey Role Models

George Clooney – grey, but sexy

Keith Richards – grey, but still
climbing coconut trees

Dame Judi Dench – grey, but
still bossing 007 about

Dame Helen Mirren – grey, but how
many men are looking at her hair?

How You Redefine Ageing

I'm not old, I'm mature – like a fine wine (no, not an old cheese!)

I'm not forgetful, I'm just more choosy about what I remember

I haven't slowed down, the
world has speeded up

I'm not a moaner, I'm a social commentator

Things Only The Young Worry About

University fees – you went to the
University of Life for nothing!

Spots – you only have to worry
about which beauty spots to visit

Having the right trainers – you are more concerned with having the left and the right trainers

Things That Are (Happily) Now Beyond Your Ken

Tablets – apart from those you take for your many ailments, of course

The Advantages Of Being Slower

Well, for a start, everything lasts longer

By the time you get to the top of
the stairs it's finally come back to
you what you went up there for

How Things Have Changed!

What You Heard Then	What You Hear Now
A cool new pop record	An infernal racket
Old people moaning in the post office queue	Sparkling conversation
Boring, middle-of-the-road music	Proper singers singing proper songs
The exciting roar of a powerful car engine	Another flipping boy racer

Excitement!

Who needs theme parks? Just
going on an escalator is a white-
knuckle ride for you, nowadays

The top speed of a mobility scooter
is 8 mph – burnin' rubber!

The sight of a slightly attractive,
middle-aged daytime TV presenter
is enough to set the pulses racing

Play chocolate box Russian roulette
with 'who'll get the hard centre first?'

Why Driving Is Better For You Now

Road signs are a bit blurry, so
why bother with them?

When you suddenly feel you are going
terrifyingly fast you realise you are
still well within the speed limit

The Icing On The Cake

You can travel free on buses –
even when you don't need to!

If you're interested in finding out more about our books, find us on Facebook at **Summersdale Publishers** and follow us on Twitter at **@Summersdale**.

www.summersdale.com